SELLING WITH AUTHORITY

Quick Reference Guide

GREGORY V. PARHAM

CONTRIBUTIONS BY DR. TIM HAVARD

Copyright © 2013 Gregory V. Parham
All rights reserved.
ISBN: 1477559396
ISBN 13: 9781477559390

CONTENTS

The Success Gene 1

Chapter 1: Defining Personal Sales 11

Chapter 2: Preparation and Strategy 23

Chapter 3: Locating and Engaging Customers. 37

Chapter 4: Discovery.......................... 53

Chapter 5: Pitch and Bargaining 67

Chapter 6: Post-Sale 81

Chapter 7: Knowledge, Skills, Abilities
         and Other Factors 95

THE SUCCESS GENE

I am going to start this book by asking you a question.

Is there such a thing as the 'Success Gene' – something in the make-up of successful people that gives them the edge over other people?

Most people would say 'yes'. We all know people in work and play for whom success seems to come with ease. They are the ones who, seem to effortlessly get the friends, who people listen to, who get the promotions or just the ear of the boss.

But is it nature or nurture?

Well this is something that has very much interested scientists. Working with twins, a leading school in the field, The University of Edinburgh has suggested that genes ARE a factor in success. The results, published in the Journal of Personality[1], revealed genes to play a much bigger role than lifestyle, with self-control particularly etched into our DNA.

---

[1] University of Edinburgh (2012, May 16). Character traits determined genetically? Genes may hold the key to a life of success, study suggests. ScienceDaily. Retrieved January 29, 2013, from http://www.sciencedaily.com/releases/2012/05/120516115903.htm

Our genes also define how determined and persistent we are. This is important in terms of success, as someone who refuses to give up is more likely to achieve their dreams than someone who throws in the towel at the first hurdle.

Is that it then? Should we just bow to the inevitability of how we are made up and just accept that some people are going to be more successful than us?

Well not necessarily. Professor Bates, who led the research, says a sense of purpose is key and advises those vying for success to focus their thoughts on making a difference.

And that is a key statement. This leading professor says that the individual can make a difference to themselves in the way they approach their lives, how they organise themselves and how they prepare.

So think again about those successful people you see around you. Is their ability to get the promotion, to get their way in business and life, and (to approach the focus of this book) to get that sale just simply down to their natural talent and inherent make-up?

Or have they worked at it?

Have they acquired the ear, the RESPECT of other, that enabled them to be listened to and thus close the deal because they had, in fact, developed the success gene themselves by the way they have prepared for that moment?

The answer is, almost certainly, yes.

Think about another, more extreme example of success in human endeavour, the Olympic games.

To be an Olympian you do have to have a natural talent, that goes without saying. However within any given

Olympic event, what lifts one individual above the others to see them crowned as champion? Certainly there are examples of supremely talented individuals, the Jesse Owens, the Bob Beamans, whose exquisite talent will lift them to the top, but the majority of competitors do not have that unfair advantage.

So what makes them a winner?

The answer is simple. It is not just turning up and competing in the hope that they might win, it is down to preparation. Preparation in every field.

In illustration (figure 1) we are going to use the five rings of the Olympics. In reality, the five rings stand for the five inhabited continents from which the competitors are drawn, but they can also stand for the five areas which the athlete has to have in place to give them a chance of winning the gold medal:

Figure 1

These are:
- Training and Fitness– the long hours the athlete puts in to ensure they are at their peak of development
- The Development of their Skills – natural talent is wasted if the key skills of your sport are not worked on
- The Psychological Development – athletes must be mentally strong, if only to believe that they are better than the people they are trying to beat
- Coaching – No modern athlete wins on their own, they need a coach to guide, to be a sounding post, to listen and advise
- Finally, they must learn to compete.

So where does this fit in with selling? This is meant to be a book about selling, isn't it? So far we have had genes and Olympic athletes.

Ah but it is all relevant.

Some people believe that there are natural salesmen who use their success gene to always close the deal. Other books, guides and many training programs of companies aimed at their sales teams just concentrate on the deal, the negotiations and the closing. They concentrate on the tricks and flim-flam that the salesperson must learn to make more sales.

The first statement is a half-truth. Yes, there are a few talented individuals out there who have the natural ability to succeed but we can guarantee that NONE of them can succeed without the proper preparation and development. This is just like an Olympian who is sure not to win if any one of the five components are not in place BEFORE they compete.

Similarly, just concentrating on the deal and the tricks is like throwing a talented young sportsman into competition without training, without a coach, and/or without the development of the mental toughness needed to win. A rare few, a very few, might come through it but we would suggest that even a Michael Phelps would drown if he had been put in that position.

But this is what happens to too many salespeople.

Our philosophy, developed through experience gained over many years and building on academic qualifications, is much more holistic, much more like the overall approach needed for the success as an Olympian. Particularly in that there is concentration on the roots of the sale, on the PREPARATION OF THE INDIVIDUAL to sell and not just on the closing of the deal. Essentially it is the process of developing the success gene in the individual.

This is **SELLING WITH AUTHORITY!**

The view of the sales process can even be fitted into the five Olympic rings! (Figure 2)

Figure 2

Just as in the preparation of an Olympic sportsman, each of these components is as important as the next. If anyone of the five is missing then the salesperson is unlikely to succeed.

It is these five components that this book is going to concentrate on, and it is more common for me to present them in our seminars in the format below and it is elements from this that we will look at in turn throughout the rest of the book:

I would stress that this is a very different approach to most 'sales' books.

Most companies teach their sales force to sell a limited range of products, similarly business/sales coaching books teach you 'tricks' and short term techniques for closing a sale. This approach is very different. What I am trying to get you to develop are deeply embedded life skills, a way of thinking that will produce more widely applicable skills that will enable the user to be able to sell anything - including yourselves.

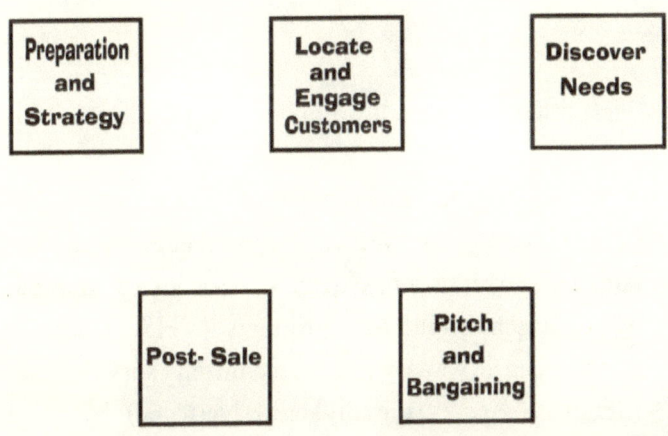

Sales and selling here are more than a narrow career description. Life is, after all, all about selling.

In a way we 'sell' ourselves throughout our lives -
- to friends
- to partners
- to prospective employers
- to business partners

We 'sell' ideas to others and other 'sell' ideas to us -
- politicians are effectively selling ideas to us - we have to have confidence in their ability to deliver on their promises/dreams that they tell us they can provide

- our own ideas to colleagues, employees and employers if we see better ways of doing things - (and achieve personal advancement)
- Neighbors, community, friends etc. to improve quality of life

And, of course, we sell products and products are sold to us -
- This may be the narrow view of selling but we still have to accept that we live in a market economy and sales make things work – there are a lot of examples where arguably inferior products (VHS, Microsoft windows and IE) have beaten technically superior ones (Betamax, Apple (initially) and Netscape) by better selling. It is also interesting to look at how Apple have hit back with a sales/desirability/fashion led approach.

So this book IS about selling but it is not a run-of-the-mill sales book. Before we get too far into this book, we want to set a few expectations.

This program, Selling With Authority, begins with this book. This book is a first step in part of a much larger universe of learning. I will promise you that upon completion of this book you will not be a Zig Ziglar, an Andy Robbins or a Chet Holmes. Actually, I will have failed you if you don't have more questions than answers upon completion of this book. However, this book will form the foundation of learning for you. You will understand the process of a sale and how things, like the way you think, affect your ability to deliver a product to a consumer.

You may not be a sales professional now and you may not aim to be one in the long term or after completion of this book.

So why are we even here?

We are here to start a process in changing the way you and I think about sales and also about life. This won't or can't happen overnight, so we are starting now and by the time you finish this program and are ready to start servicing your customers, you will be professional, sophisticated, and provided the tools to be successful, not just in the narrow field of sales but in your life generally.

In short I aim to give you the success gene – or at least enable you to give the impression to others that you have it!

CHAPTER 1

DEFINING PERSONAL SALES

- This chapter will look at the key concepts of Selling With Authority
- We will spend quite a bit of time looking at DEFINITIONS so we all know exactly what we are talking about and what we mean when we use certain terms
- At the end of this chapter you should how the paradigm of personal sales fits into your role as a salesperson

---

Everyone knows what we mean by the term 'Sale' – don't they? Sales and selling is something that we all experience almost every day of our lives. If we really want to we can look up a definition of sales – there are plenty of definitions as to what a sale is, which include -

sale (sl)[2]

n.

1. The exchange of goods or services for an amount of money or its equivalent; the act of selling.
2. An instance of selling.
3. An opportunity for selling or being sold; demand.
4. Availability for purchase: a store where pets are for sale.
5. A selling of property to the highest bidder; an auction.
6. A special disposal of goods at lowered prices: coats on sale this week.
7. sales
   a. Activities involved in selling goods or services.
   b. Gross receipts.

This, however, is not the definition that we will be using throughout this book. We will be using a simpler but more fundamental definition:

An Exchange Between Parties

This does look deceptively simple but it is our contention that this is an art that most professional sales people and the people who train them have failed to master and as result often tend to achieve sub-optimal results. The typical salesperson misses the simplicity of this concept and focuses on techniques that are either more complicated

---

[2] Source: The Free on-Line Dictionary

Defining Personal Sales

than necessary or require experience that the salesperson lacks (a salesperson who identifies this typically goes out and researches sales techniques because they acknowledge that they lack experience).

This seems to be a very sweeping statement. However, as you progress through the book, you will come to understand why we strongly believe this to be the case.

But why do we use a definition that doesn't actually mention a monetary transaction, the sale of goods or services, indeed any of the 'hard' or 'real' aspects of selling mentioned in the dictionary definition?

The reason is quite simple; this book is about more than the simple act of the sale. This definition is about personal sales and selling. So what is Personal Sales?

As we mentioned in the introduction, sales are far more important to our lives than the simple, narrow definition of selling and sales given above. All the time we sell and are sold to, even when there is no actual monetary exchange involved. We sell ourselves to others all the time, we sell ideas and concepts, and others sell the same to us, be they our nearest and dearest or those located in Washington D.C., the state capital or our local city hall.

You can see that what is happening is an exchange of ideas and information. This is happening all the time.

Do we always accept that exchange, do we believe everything that is put to us and, in turn, is every idea, concept and position that we offer accepted? Clearly the answer is no. How we distinguish between what we are willing to accept and what we are not is how believable what we are being told is and how much respect we have for the person delivering it.

Consider this scenario: a wild-eyed, dishevelled man dashes into an office's reception shouting that there is a fire and everyone should get out. Would everyone pay attention to him? Would they all get up and leave? Okay, now let's change things: the man who rushes in is a firefighter, full uniform, helmet, radio shouting the same thing. This time it is pretty certain that everyone will do as they are told. Why? The firefighter has respect. He hasn't actually provided any more information than the man who dashed in from the street (who may well be dishevelled because he has sprinted three blocks to warn his fellow human beings of danger!) yet, without proof he is believed. (This can work to the detriment of people: In the 2011 massacre of young political activists on an island in Norway, the young people actually ran to the killer, Anders Brevik, because he was wearing a police uniform.)

What we are doing every day is forming value judgements, often because we have no other choice, dependent on how much respect we have for the person delivering the message. Do they know what they are talking about? Are they believable? Do they have an ulterior motive or are they being genuine?

This is where we get back to sales. Sales in the narrow sense, the monetary sense that salespersons, trainers and their companies get rather naturally fixated on.

It is our contention that most salespersons fail because they do not understand this definition and what it really means. We believe that sales people often lack respect from their potential customers because they cannot demonstrate the depth of knowledge that they need to convince. This leads either to a failure to sell or, and often this is worse, a failure to sell optimally.

Why this is viewed as being worse is because a sale is made even before the customer has met the salesperson. The salesperson is not able to help the customer because the customer simply does not respect them. A salesman in this situation is being treated more like a human version of a vending machine. They might just shrug and just say 'a sale is a sale, I've done my job' but what they are doing (and the company is allowing them to do) is potentially damaging the business. If customers come to believe that a retailer is self-service (ie: like a vending machine), the opportunity to sell complimentary products that the customer might not know they need or could enhance their experience is virtually nil. Also, if a customer has a lackluster experience that leads to a return because they have been sold the wrong product, then the trust in the retailer is damaged permanently, even if the customer gave them no opportunity to explore their real needs. An example of this can arguably be seen in Best Buy; early on, it performed very well, but prolonged brand damage due to a failure to sell optimally has caused many locations to close and the company to near bankruptcy.

Concentrating on the personal sales definition, the idea that the point of sale is only the outcome of a richer exchange of ideas and information is the root of this new paradigm of personal selling. The Oxford English Dictionary defines the basic meaning of the term paradigm as "a pattern or model, an exemplar" and that really sums up what this book is all about; it gives you a pattern to follow that should improve your ability to sell – and not just goods and services but in every aspect of your life.

In other words you should be able to sell salesperson more successfully.

You may read books on the science of sales, psychology of sales, influence tactics and more, but there is something that no book can ever teach you: the art of performing a sale. This book isn't different in that sense. You will not be an expert outside salesperson when you finish. You will, however, have a new way of looking at sales that encourages learning more on the topics. Self-discovery and self-analysis are things that every master salesperson has. They understand their strengths and weaknesses and can determine what to focus their resources on improving.

Before we go further and explore the different types of sales situations that exist (taking the narrow definition of selling here).

How much you will gain in immediate terms from the program depends upon which situation you currently work in.

There are all types of salespeople out there, and most are a combination of sales types. We have broken salespeople down into three categories for the purposes of this program:

Inside Salespeople

The inside salesperson is unique in that they do not go outside of the business to seek customers. Typically, customers come to the business either physically or via electronic means.

This type of salesperson is expected to perform well in this type of environment, and requires a unique set of skills for dealing with their customers. Imagine, if you don't control how often a customer comes your way, how much pressure are you under to close every sale possible? The inside salesperson handles this type of pressure daily.

Inside salespeople typically are customer service oriented which encourages customers to return for more business, are expected to offer as much to a customer as is practical, and are able to quickly make a connection with a customer.

Is this profile already sounding familiar? If you go to the mall, you may see this type of salesperson working in your retail stores, or if you call into your wireless phone provider's customer support lines, you may hear this person assist you then offer a new service.

Outside Salespeople

Outside salespeople are charged with looking outside of a business to find new customers for their products or services. The term "business development" is a fun way of saying "outside salespeople try to reach new customers."

There is a stigma that typically follows an outside salesperson. Outside salespeople are often seen as nuisances or pesky cold callers and not as the important piece of the commerce puzzle that they are! A company that creates a new product needs people to go into the market and advocate it. How does a customer even know that a new product or service is available unless someone reaches out to share information? Outside salespeople need to be able to go to the customer to facilitate trade.

Sure, some of the tactics of outside salespeople are bothersome at times, but that does not detract from the important role they play for a business.

> **REFLECTION POINT:**
>
> What type of salesperson are you?
>
> To define who you are, you need to look at your roles as a salesperson. Which roles sound like you? Are you a combination? This will be important when determining how to look at the sales processes later in this book.

Indirect Salespeople

Not all salespeople deal with the customer or end user of a product or service. When was the last time a pharmaceutical salesperson wrote a prescription for a patient?

The indirect salesperson is a master of persuasion and influence. This type of salesperson is expected to interface with the parties responsible for the direct sale of their product or service to improve the likelihood that their product or service gets sold. The term "mind-share" is often used to describe how much influence an indirect salesperson has with a party.

To achieve these goals, an indirect salesperson positively positions their products and services, leverages compliance and persuasion tactics (which is an advanced concept), trains parties on the products or services and is a point of contact between a business and a distribution point.

Now that you have reflected on the type of salesperson-salesperson you are and the type of environment you work in, we need to look at another important area; filters and lenses.

We will be referring to filters and lenses a lot throughout this book so it is another important definition to establish and understand.

What we are essentially talking about here is how people see things. What is their view or perspective on something?

If you watch any films or TV shows you will be familiar with the effect of this. Film makers use different lenses and filters to give the effect that they want. Those vast, panoramic views, the moody, dark skies on an otherwise clear day or bold, vivid, almost unreal colors are not achieved by waiting for just the right light or atmospheric conditions, but instead by using different lenses and filters. Very little of what we actually see on-screen is 'real' or unenhanced.

Lenses and filters are subtlety different. A lens determines the view we see; either wide-angled, giving the broader picture, or else a zoom or telephoto lens that allows us to see the detail. The filter sits in front of the lens and alters the picture we see. In terms of our day-to-day lives and work, a filter is about how you interpret information given to you.

We filter information all of the time, but becoming aware of how to filter will be critical throughout a sales process. When dealing with objections, you will need to filter certain things to identify, for example, if the customer really has an issue with what you are saying or if they are just trying to get rid of you or make their escape.

We need to learn to zoom onto the points that matter most. This is incredibly important during discovery as you may get more information from a customer than what is necessary to recommend a solution. A salesperson should isolate and fix onto the key issues.

Now let us look at lenses and filters in the context of this book. If we ask you to look at something through the customer's lens, we are asking you to step out of your current thought process and think from a different perspective. If we ask you to put on the "what's in it for me" filter, we want you to think about what's the value proposition in what you are thinking.

Putting it Together

It is important to note that Selling with Authority is not about gaining an upper-hand on those we sell to. Nothing could be further from the truth: We believe that sales are most effective (and most beneficial) when they are based on a desire to serve. We call this the "attitude of service."

You have a moral imperative to use these skills to improve the situation of both you and your customer instead of just you. If you are agreeable to this, please join us as we dive into the how behind a sale.

Now that we have the broadest sense possible of what a sale is, let's break it down into the components that we will discuss chapter by chapter. If you read other books (which we highly encourage), you may see this same process called something different, or have different terminology. However, for this book and course, we will use the following terminology.

Step 1: Preparation and Strategy
Step 2: Locate and Engage Customers
Step 3: Discovery
Step 4: Pre-Sale
Step 5: Post-Sale
Step 6: Knowledge, Skills, Abilities and Other Factors for All Phases

Every sale will have each step used to some degree. A simple exchange at your local grocery store for batteries includes all of these steps. A step may last a fraction of a second or last several weeks. Regardless, we all need to be aware of all of these steps and find ways to improve our performance through their use.

CHAPTER 2

PREPARATION AND STRATEGY

- In this chapter we will look at a key concept in Selling with Authority; preparation and strategy
- At the end of this chapter you will have an understanding of relationships, communication and respect in the sales process
- We will show how good preparation is essential in breaking down the respect barriers between customer and salespersonsalesperson

---

We start this chapter with a question; what is the most important part of a sale?

Would it surprise you that the most important part of a sale isn't collecting on an exchange? The most important part of a sale is what we do before we even speak to our first customer: it's the preparation we do beforehand.

We prepare for almost everything we do. Making dinner, getting well dressed for an interview, studying for a test and cleaning the house for a guest are all examples of how we prepare for things. The Boy Scouts of America believe being prepared is highly important. It's their motto.

If you look at other sales books or have attended sales courses before, we think you will find that most sales models do not count the preparation and strategy as a part of the model. This is where we differ so much from other approaches, we view it as critical. Most sales models follow a similar pattern, but very few include preparation and strategy as a part of the sales process.

So what do we mean by preparation and strategy in the context of selling? Well, it's what we do before the sale. We argue that it's the most important part. It is the part that runs throughout the process and where the vast majority of Selling with Authority takes place. The actual sale in the transaction is only a point in the overall scheme.

Why we feel this is important requires a careful examination of sale situations and, most importantly, the communication that occurs in this process and the status and respect accorded to the salespersonsalesperson.

We'll start with this diagram (figure 2.1):-

Figure 2.1

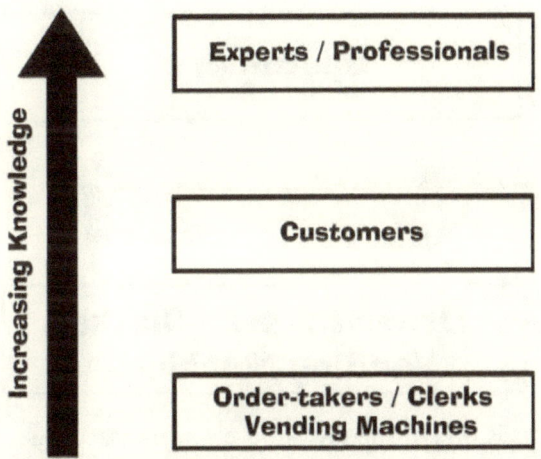

What we are going to look at is the contrasting relationships and communication that takes place in the polar opposite sales situations.

Starting at the bottom part of the diagram, we will look at the relationship between customers and order takers (figure 2.2).

Figure 2.2

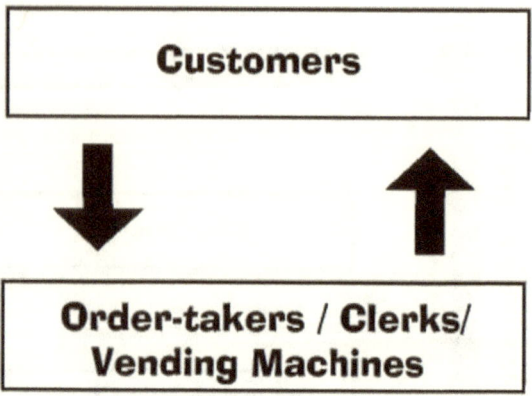

This is one of the lowest levels of transactions.

It is helpful to view this through the customers' lens, the concept that we mentioned in the previous chapter. We want to see this relationship from their viewpoint. In the customer and order taker situation, the customer does not expect to see the person before them as someone who is going to be much to help to them, beyond filling the order. In most cases, the customer will typically have done research before they come in. Effectively they know what they want – or they think they do, but it is quite possible the solution they have chosen is not the one that best meets their need. In the 'lens' of the customer, the order taker is merely the means of achieving that end.

Because their default position is that the person who serves them is not going to be able to help them, they will not be receptive to someone who challenges this position. Challenging the customer is how to break out of this scenario. The default answer to an offer is 'no' because the customer perceives themselves to have more knowledge than the order taker. The question that a customer asks themselves in reaction to an offer is 'should I accept this offer?' Since the customer has the perception of more knowledge, and didn't come in asking for what is being offered, the chances of them accepting is very slim.

Corporations are well aware of the situation. In many cases, the order taker has been able to be replaced by a machine. Consider a vending machine; this provides exactly the same function as an order taker fulfills for the customer. It is merely there to deliver something that the customer has chosen without any input from the machine itself. To some extent, this also applies to online retailing. Best Buy now has vending machines that sell expensive electronics in airports because of how 'robotic' the purchase of consumer electronics has become (Figure 2.3).

Figure 2.3

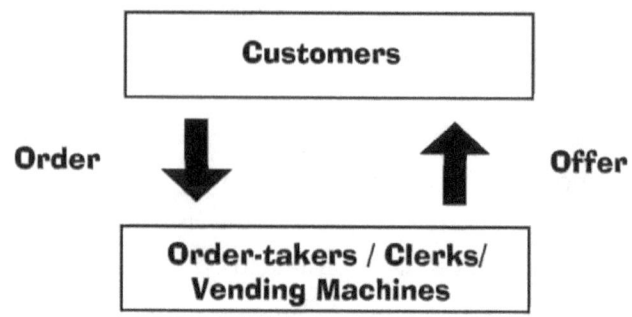

The situation places the order taker in a very difficult position. There is little they can do to perform better to add value to the sales process. All they can do is try to make offers -
- 'Would you like this as well...?'
- 'Have you tried...?'
- 'Today you can add...'

This is a terrible way to offer a product/service to a customer, a customer who is already resistant to any input from the salesperson! The customer has brought low expectations to the process and is convinced that salesperson knows less than they do.

Essentially there is a lack of respect in this relationship. The customer has little respect for the salesperson. This is unlikely to be expressed by the customer being rude or insulting to the salesperson – though those working in telesales or cold calling might beg to differ! - but more commonly in an in-built resistance to listening to information and offers that might well be useful to them!

Preparation and Strategy

Now let us look at a different sales relationships, again using our main diagram. What we are going to look at is the customer - expert relationship.

The dynamics in this relationship are entirely different.

An expert is, by their very definition, acknowledged as having particular expertise in their field. Customers will go to them because they want information from this expert regarding ways of meeting the customer's needs, wants, goals and wishes. The expert can ask questions of the customer to better judge what they need. In fact that is just why the customer has gone to them. In addition, customers are more open to answering questions posed by an expert because there is a respect and understanding that the information they are gathering will be put to good use.

This puts the expert in a very advantageous position.

Experts are expected to ask questions; therefore they are even able to ask open-ended questions - effectively questions that are fishing for information - as well as closed-end questions that enables the salesperson to move towards closing the deal.

The customer in this situation asks very different sorts of questions from that in the customer – order taker relationship-
- 'what do you think...?'
- 'How does that sound? Do you think it will do the job for me...?'
- 'What do I need to...?'

This only works if the customer perceives the seller as being an expert --an expert who has more product knowledge and, perhaps in addition, knowledge about the customer's needs.

This implies that product knowledge in training is essential. This is because the salesperson must demonstrate mastery of the product/services which they are selling or delivering. The expert is looked on by the customer as somebody who can make a recommendation, someone who can tell the customer what they need to fulfill their needs and therefore solve their problem.

We think that most people will be able to see the big attraction of this; the sale is essentially assured. Price is not the big obstacle, usually affording a product or service is. Instead of a customer asking should I buy, they're now asking how do I afford it?

There is an obvious conclusion: the key thing for a salesperson (and the company they work for) is to move from being an order taker towards being an expert.

One way of achieving this, as we have already seen, is the preparation and in-depth training in the product or service you are selling. This may, depending on the circumstances, mean looking more widely at the needs of the main customers. What do they need the product or service for, what are they trying to do? Above all, what problems or challenges do they face and how does your product or service provide a solution?

That is the preparation but what about the strategy? (Bearing in mind, of course, that preparation is part of the strategy!) How do you get the message over to the customer if their chosen lens gives them a default position of 'not listening'?

The goal of the salesperson is to identify the default stance of the customer when they first come into contact with them. You must identify whether they are pro-or anti-seller, whether they're expecting an order taker or an expert? Certain industries have particularly strong perceptions about them. Car part sellers are perceived as order takers (and there really is very little upselling that they can do), but they are very well trained in the inner workings of cars. Focusing on the perception of the industry as a whole is a great place to start.

> **REFLECTION POINT:**
>
> Can you think of examples of experts in the sales process?
>
> It's probably easy to think of specialist examples of 'experts' – pharmaceutical representatives who visit doctor's surgeries, or sellers of specialist software packages – but what about in more general retailing? Are there any major retailers who set up their sales teams in this way?

If the customer is an anti-seller the salesmen must act to try to change this mindset.

The signs as to what type the customer is are fairly straightforward. Firstly, if the customer does not ask the order taker's opinion on the product or service then that is a pretty clear sign that they are just expecting to deal with an order taker. You should also look at the customer's body language; is it resistant? Do they give off the signs that they are closed and defensive?

To break the mindset of the anti-seller, the salesperson must show them that they are an expert. This is not easy if the customer is not expecting it, but if you can show that you know things that they don't (but avoiding the superior 'tech-speak' that too many in certain industries fall into), that you really understand their needs, perhaps even perceiving them better than the customer themselves know them, then you will start to make progress. The sophisticated salesperson knows how to strike a balance between personability and jargon.

When you achieve this you should see the customer's body language relax, their interest becomes piqued, and they become more interested in the product and services offered and about the views expressed by you, the salesperson. They may even start guiding you to closing. If you are selling with authority, the customer should naturally see that your product and/or service is beginning to solve their problems and will thus lead themselves toward a close.

The key thing is to persuade the customer of the difference between a cashier and the salesperson. And the best way to do that is preparation – knowing your product and the market.

Hopefully you will see how this holistic approach makes the individual parts of the sale easier.

In the second part of this chapter we will look at some practical things that you can do to improve your chances of fulfilling the expert role in the sales process.

Your Individual Business Plan

Earlier in this book, we asked you to take a break and look at yourself as different kinds of salespeople. This is another exercise similar to before, except right now, we want you to evaluate yourself as a salesperson.

Look at yourself holistically and evaluate your level of business acumen, salesmanship skills, persuasiveness, or any and all factors you think are relevant to your success as a salesperson. Only you know what affects your ability to close a sale. If having confidence is important, evaluate it. If how well you groom yourself is affecting sales, evaluate it. Get creative, because there are thousands of factors that can affect a sale, and we cannot list each one out for you. We challenge you to come up with at least 20 factors, but don't go beyond 40. These factors are what you are going to focus on in your individual business plan.

Your individual business plan is going to be your road map for self-improvement over the next several weeks and months. It can be a formal document you compose in a word processor, a chart you draw or even a contract with yourself. However you choose, you need to make sure that it has SMART goals in it. A SMART goal is:

Specific – what EXACTLY are you going to improve?

Measurable – how will you measure progress in your improvement?

Actionable – what specific actions will you take to improve each factor?

Resourced – what tools do you have to make the improvements to each factor?

Time-bound - how often will you revisit your progress or what deadlines have you set?

For a real estate agent, one might want to improve prospecting skills. To measure success, that agent may see success if leads increase by 10%. To improve, that agent may enroll in a prospecting webinar for real estate agents. That agent may use the internet, other agents and friends as resources. That agent would want to see an improvement in 30 days.

This is an example of a SMART goal. Your business plan should have at least 20 of these (at least 1 per factor identified). This plan can be modified at any time to remove mastered factors or to add factors that you identify as being important through your learning steps.

There are a few things to remember in this process. The first one is to do things in easy stages. If you were setting out to eat an elephant you wouldn't do it at one sitting! You can't change or improve everything at once; small incremental stages are much more likely to succeed.

The second is to be honest with yourself. We probably have all made resolutions and then failed to keep them. To succeed with the SMART goals and your personal business plan you do need to be both diligent and honest with yourself about keeping to your program.

One last thing we want everyone to put in their individual business plan is a way to include a support system.

"No man is an island." – John Donne

This quote is a great way for us to say that every salesperson needs a support system to help improve their skills and knowledge. A support system should include mentors and practice partners.

There are two kinds of mentors, and both are important to have. A "horizontal mentor" is a mentor that shares the same position or comparable position as you. This could be a salesperson from the same company, a competitor or someone in another line of sales, but who does the same type of work as you. A "vertical mentor" is a superior (not necessarily your own) who you can call upon to help you drive your development. Vertical mentorship is fairly uncommon and not because the mentor is too busy. Often, people are nervous or afraid to even ask. You'd be shocked at where your career could be if you simply reached out to people in superior positions!

Practice partners are also important people to have in your individual business plan. These are the people you will be speaking to regularly to improve and fine tune your pitches and sales skills. You should be comfortable with this person to call them up and say "I have a new pitch I want to run by you. Could you give me some feedback on it?"

The goal, of course, is to practice on someone who can give meaningful feedback without practicing on a customer! We all have wanted to be a pro athlete at some point or another. Glory, fame and money are all very attractive things! However, we don't think about what happens off the field. A professional football player (American) will spend 5 days a week in practice just to play an hour long game on Saturday. We don't imagine ourselves doing the hard work that goes behind the success!

As you can see, this step of the sales process is very important. You need to always be preparing for the next sales opportunity. Whether that involves learning more about the products and services you sell, identifying areas of opportunity with yourself, or fine tuning your sales model, you will be spending a lot of time working on your preparation and strategy.

This part is mostly "on your honor" in that it is very hard to verify that you are doing these steps. Regardless, these are the most important of all. If you aren't seeking improvement, you aren't becoming a better salesperson. Don't sell yourself short on this step!

CHAPTER 3

LOCATING AND ENGAGING CUSTOMERS

- In this chapter we will look at the next stage in Selling With Authority – locating and engaging customers
- The differences between outside and inside sales people are highlighted
- The main concentration is on engaging customers – making a good first impression, breaking the ice and getting yourself established as an authority with the customer

---

This very important pair of factors in the sales process have to be considered together. They are a distinct and critical phase in achieving a sale. Customers have to be found and then contact made with them to start the dialogue that should, hopefully, lead the salesperson to finding out what the customer needs and closing the sale. However we will spend more time on the second rather than the first.

You may be asking; why?

It is obvious that the sales process takes place in a number of different ways in often quite different environments.

The salesperson's job can be looked at as a spectrum, a range of different activities. On one extreme is the pure outside salesperson. The outside salesperson spends all of their time actively seeking customers. The opposite of this is a purely inside salesperson who wait for the customers to come to them. Inside salespeople are epitomized by the inbound tele-salesperson. (Try consulting Wikipedia for their take on inside salespeople.)

The outside salesperson depends upon lead generation -- in fact often they create the leads for themselves, hunting out customers to sell to. The inside salesperson relies on advertising and marketing to attract customers into their place of work, be it a shop for the sale of a product or an office where a service is being supplied.

It is very rare for someone to be based entirely outside or entirely inside, most people's jobs are a range of different types, a mixture, with some work time being spent outside and some inside.

> **REFLECTION POINT:**
>
> What is your job like? Are you more of an outside salesperson or an inside one?

Because of these varying types and because leads are generated or marketing carried out in different ways for different industries, it is very hard to produce rules and tips that are specific enough to be useful to the majority of salespersons reading this book.

There are a number of other sources and books that concentrate only on marketing, advertising and lead generation. Most are industry specific! This book would become dominated by material on this section if we covered it in depth. What we are trying to focus on here, however, is the overall process that will lead to closing a deal. We want to concentrate on the one-to-one relationship between you as a salesperson and the prospective customer. For this reason will not be spending any more time on the process of locating customers but now will home in on the second part of the process -- engaging the customer.

Engaging the Customer

The First Contact

It is an important fact to understand that your first contact with a customer starts well before you, as a salesperson, even utter your first word.

There is a rather hackneyed saying; 'You never get a second chance to make a first impression'. It may be an old phrase but it has survived the test of time because it happens to be true.

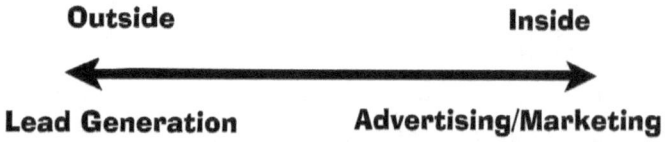

Outside — **Lead Generation**
Inside — **Advertising/Marketing**

It is time to adopt the view, the lens, of the customer again.

Think of what they are going to see when they make first contact with you.

If they are coming into your place of work they will see a lot of things before they see you. They will see your company's signage, they may see the products that you are selling; they will definitely see where you are working. Is it tidy, does it project the right image? Is there anything in it that might offend the customer in some way or put them in the wrong state of mind? All of these things must be considered or else the customer might already be resistant to any approach you make. This is where stepping into the potential customer's shoes will really help you to consider the small details that could be the difference between a successful sale and them going elsewhere. Top retailers have strict merchandising rules and cleanliness rules to ensure a uniformly excellent experience for the customer.

If they have gotten past the impression that your place of work presents (or you an outside salesperson) then the next 'first' impression is of you yourself.

How you carry yourself on the job dictates how your customers will perceive your work (and sales) value. If you are in a uniform , or generally smartly dressed and are professional and neat then you are going to make a good first impression. But it goes beyond just the way you are dressed and whether you are well groomed or not. If you are lounging around the shop or office, if you have poor posture then you will come over as being unprofessional and uninterested. Again this will raise barriers between you and the potential customer.

Another thing to remember is that engagement takes place with all the customer's senses. Don't just concentrate on the visual cues and neglect the other four senses -

- **Visual engagement** - Cell phone stores use lots of high tech looking materials and lights to attract customers and make a statement of what they are about. High end clothing stores are built to be stylish and trendy. We form our first impression of the product from the moment we see these sights.
- **Auditory engagement** - Who can forget the ice cream man? That sound from streets over would have his customers waiting by the curb for when he arrived, which

is the sign of a very astute businessman. It's not the only example: Music is typically played in retail stores to keep customers engaged while salespeople are busy. Music also acts to position the brand in the mind of the customers; those stores playing the latest hot acts that might irritate the parents are telling the teenage customers that this is the place to buy the latest fashions. Ever wondered why there is music when you're holding on the phone? It is to maintain engagement.

- **Olfactory engagement** - Movie theaters use the smell of popcorn to entice patrons over to the sales point to get snacks. Abercrombie and Fitch hoses their sales floor with perfume for that unique smell while browsing for clothes. Real Estate specialists advise that the smell of fresh coffee and newly baked bread cause potential buyers to associate the properties they are viewing with "home" and make a bid more likely.
- **Taste engagement** - The most obvious example of these are free samples! Who doesn't like free samples of treats or food? Generosity is only so much - that taste typically leaves you wanting more. You find yourself with a problem to solve that you didn't have a few moments before. Costco is particularly good at this – especially as they sell in larger quantities.
- **Kinetic engagement** - Salespeople love kinetic engagement. Touch. A solid handshake, a pat on the shoulder. This forms a particularly strong form of engagement; humans use touch to bond with those that are close to us. Being able to handle a product, to feel its quality,

how nice it is to use also gives the customer this kinetic engagement. This is something heavily used in Apple stores.

If you remember from the previous chapter, your goal should be to get in a position to display your product knowledge and be viewed as expert, someone with authority. To be able to be established as that it is important to get to a point where the customer will listen to you. The preparation that you make beforehand is critical. Even if the day is quiet and slow, be prepared to receive that next customer – remembering that opportunity to make that first impression may only be a moment away. From the moment your customer identifies you, you are engaged in communication with the customer. Therefore, your first impression may occur even before you realize there is a customer present.

This overlaps with another key communication rule.

The 55-38-7 Rule

Professor Albert Mehrabian, Ph.D., of the University of California, Los Angles (UCLA), is credited as the originator of the 55%, 38%, 7% Rule. He and his colleagues conducted two studies on communication patterns and published the studies in professional journals in 1967.

Mehrabian published the results of his work in two books, Silent Messages (Wadsworth Publishing, 1971) and Nonverbal Communications (Aldine Atherton, Inc., 1972). In these books Mehrabian suggests that body language and tonality are, perhaps, a more accurate indicator of emotions and meaning than the words themselves.

This gives the general guide that communication is made up of 55% physical cues, 38% tone and 7% words. Although some people have criticized how applicable this is in general communication, it is important to remember that HOW you say something and WHAT your body language is will effect how the words you say are received.

You cannot fake interest in the customer - your non-verbal cues WILL betray how you really feel. Therefore, it is critically important to actually be in the field you want to work in. If you are unhappy, your customers will be able to detect it.

It's also important to be congruent when we communicate. That is, our body language and tone of voice should be consistent with the words we use. Otherwise we can confuse people and reduce the prospect of getting our message across so that it is understoodAs a seller, your job is to perform your work function. To be successful, your job is to perform your work function as best you can. Mastery of your perception from others is the FIRST STEP in doing this, so again it is important, particularly at this first step, to try to see what your customer sees.Making a strong first impression is crucially important to setting the expectation with customers that they will be buying.

Getting Beyond the First Impression

Obviously your goal should be to build on this good first impression. To do that you now need to start the verbal communication. The key thing is to get the customer to talk. This is critical.

Customers should do the majority of the talking. As a salesperson, you are not psychic nor know what your customer needs before they tell you. Customer's need to tell you what they want to buy or identify the problems they are facing.

Remember -
Listening before pitching makes you a consultant
Pitching before listening makes you a salesperson

It is the consultant's role that you should be aiming to achieve. It is this that makes selling easier and more successful.

Of course though, you cannot just wait for the customer to make the first move. It is important to find a way of breaking the ice, getting the dialogue going.

The Icebreaker

We all have made a friend at some point or another, and most likely, their desire to continue talking to us was based upon the first impression that we made. Think about how you make friends. This is not far removed from making sales! Most people like doing business with friendly people, so as a salesperson, we should approach our customers like we approach a friend. Keep that in mind.

The icebreaker is something that we say when we initiate our first contact with a new customer. Make it fun, but keep it appropriate for the kind of business you are in. We don't have many pointers regarding this because it varies based on the kind of sales you are engaged in; however, adding humor is generally accepted. For an inside salesperson, you may say something fun like "so which stereo are you going to buy from me today?" The way you say this is important because you don't want to pressure the customer at first contact, but allowing for a humorous interpretation, could be interpreted as "you know I'm a salesperson, but I can be light and fun to talk to."

A good icebreaker should build instant rapport with a customer. Rapport is going to be an important consideration throughout the sales process because without rapport, making a sale could prove difficult. People do business with salespeople they like. If a customer doesn't like you, odds are, that customer will go somewhere else that they can get what they are looking for.

> **REFLECTION POINT:**
>
> Non-visual types of engagement are often neglected by salespeople but are subtle and powerful. Can you think of some non-visual ways that are used in your workplace? And can you think of any you might use?

Compliments are good Icebreakers; people generally love compliments however be cautious; they must come over as genuine and they shouldn't be ones that could be misconstrued!

It is good to have a few 'stock' or 'go to' questions or comments in your armory. Don't worry about repeating yourself, each new customer is someone different and they do not know what you have said to other people.

> **REFLECTION POINT:**
>
> Spend a few minutes thinking up different icebreaker questions that you could use in different situations. Why might some work and some might not?

So what makes a good icebreaker question? Essentially they can be anything however they SHOULD -
- Lead on somewhere, they should encourage the start of a conversation
- Establish a rapport with the other person

They SHOULD NOT
- annoy or insult your customer in some way
- undermine the impression of professionalism and authority that you have spent so much time creating
- be closed questions that the customer can give a single answer to that will stop the conversation there!

These points are very important. Today's politicians are often criticized as being all about image. The big successful corporations spend millions of dollars on PR to present and protect a certain image about themselves. Despite this, most people are astute; they can quickly lose faith in something if the image that they have been sold turns out to be rather different from the reality. A customer may be impressed by the first sight of your place of work. They may then have this feeling reinforced by the first sight of you; well presented, smart and alert with open, honest and friendly body language. This can all come crashing down if, when you open your mouth, you come over as an annoying, boorish fool.

This is a hard balance to achieve but if you spend time considering things through your customer's lens, to stand in their shoes and see how things appear to them from their viewpoint, then you will almost certainly have a better understanding of what you need to do.

One way to develop this important area is to use your mentors. Ask them how they would react to certain icebreaker questions, whether they think they are good ones. No one can ever know (or expected to know) everything . We are all limited by our experiences. We learn best by sharing experiences and the knowledge of other people. You will almost certainly learn from your mentor's experiences and you may be surprised to find that they learn from yours! Don't be shy about asking.

Another thing to try is applying your icebreaker questions outside a selling situation, in a normal day-to-day life. One of the themes that we established earlier is that we constantly 'sell' ourselves throughout life. Why not try to start a conversation in a queue at the cinema, or at the mall or wherever? If it achieves nothing else it will give you practice in talking to strangers! It could however give you important lessons in what works and what doesn't for different types of people.

However just getting people to talk is only the start. The conversation has to go somewhere meaningful and to do that you need to do something very important, and do it early.

Establish Your Authority

During your first contact with a customer, you want to establish your authority through your expertise. The earlier you let your customer know that you are an expert, a professional and an authority on the product or service you are selling, the less actual "selling" you will have to do.

How do we mean? Customers want to speak to people with expertise and authority. While you, the salesperson, may be a charming individual, customers often want to make a purchase and continue on with their business.

To you, the sale and your product may be the most important thing in your world. Remember your customers have other priorities -

- For a major purchase for a major corporation, being involved with a purchase means that an executive must take time away from their core business.
- For a family making a major purchase, that family wants to get back home to enjoy their time together

rather than sit at a big box retailer for hours deciding on which TV to buy.

A professional and an expert will be perceived by a customer as someone who is able to make better use of their time. They will be listened to more than someone who isn't well versed in the product or service in question and is perceived as someone who will not waste their time.

So how do you establish your "authority?"

It can be summed up in one word: confidence. You must be confident in the product knowledge and understand how the customer sees the product or service you have to offer.

You can control the perception that customers have of you by offering information and insights the customer may not have had on their own. For instance, a customer can conduct research on home theater equipment online, however, that customer cannot compare the actual sound quality over the internet. By coming to a retail location and having a salesperson describe, intelligently, how to compare equipment, that salesperson has effectively demonstrated to the customer that they posses expertise beyond that of the customer.

Establishing authority does not take much time. Often, presenting an intelligent yet new view on a subject or product is enough to convince a customer that you are knowledgeable about whatever it is that you are selling. Be warned, however, that failure to demonstrate sufficient product knowledge or sophistication will almost certainly eliminate any opportunity you may have with a customer.

Furthermore, you could even run the risk of damaging your company's image by coming across as incorrect or uneducated on your product or service!

You are probably starting to see some common threads running through these chapters. That is not surprising, the whole point about Selling with Authority is that it is a holistic approach to selling. Everything is interlinked, every part is important. You can't come over as an expert with the preparation that gives you the product and market knowledge, but you will not be able to get over that knowledge to your customer if you can't engage them in a meaningful dialogue and you cannot get there if you don't make a good first impression...and so on. We could make myriad linkages throughout the process.

Each part is as important as the other.

CHAPTER 4

DISCOVERY

- In this chapter we will look at the next stage in the process of Selling with Authority – discovering the customer's needs
- This will require the development of two key skills – effective questioning and effective listening
- At the end of the chapter you will understand the difference between open and closed questions and know when it is best to use each type
- You should also appreciate the difference between passive and active listening and the role this plays in understanding the customer's need

---

We will start this chapter with a visualization of what you should be trying to achieve with this part of the sales process (Figure 4.1).

Essentially what you are trying to do is gather data, process it and then focus on the solution that you can provide for the customer -

Figure 4.1 – The Discovery Process enables the salesperson to move towards the sale

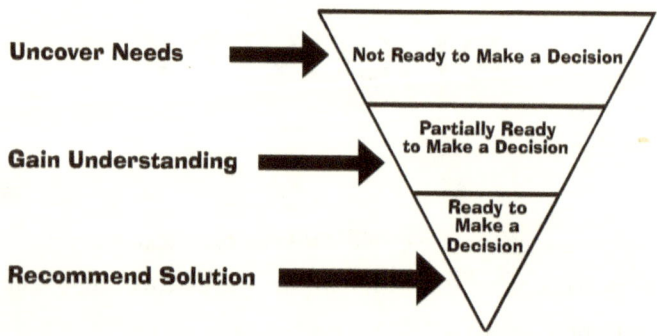

Now that you have started a conversation, and started the process of establishing yourself as an expert you now need to move on and determine the customer's needs. This is an essential step towards securing the most effective sale but also the customer will infer your expertise by the quality of question and insights gathered from effective information gathering.

To do this you must master two contrasting skills – asking questions and listening to responses. These two skills are actually in conflict with each other – no one can listen and talk at the same time. They also contrast to what you have just done in the last stage when you were trying to establish your position as expert. The key thing is that -

Discovery

Experts talk very little but, when they do, they do so with authority.

It is important therefore to let the other party to do the majority of the talking. However their talking must be used by you to its best effect -- the more information you have, the better position you will be in to know how to meet the customer's needs. The more you can see how best you can meet the customer's needs the closer you are to achieving the optimum sale.

You must therefore be skilled at both asking questions and also skilled at listening. Getting the balance between the two is hard but they are both equally important in this stage of the process.

We will ask you to view things through a customer's lens again for a moment.

Consider how annoying this conversation would be if you were the customer --

You: "Hey, I'd like to see the menu, please."
Waiter: "We have chicken on special today, Do you like chicken?"
You: "Thanks, but I'd like to see the menu."
Waiter: "We also have some delicious surf and turf combos. How does that sound?"
You: "Well I'm sure that's fine but actually I'm a vegetarian."
Waiter: "How about one of our succulent, all-you-can-eat burgers with all the trimmings. Do you like burgers? Ours are the best."

You will see that the waiter (salesperson) is pushing the things they were asked to by their manager (or the company), and that they are asking questions, but the questions are irrelevant and they are not listening to the replies. They are not finding out their customer's wants and not meeting their needs. They are likely not to end up with a sale (or tip!) but rather with a severely antagonized customer who will most likely walk out.

This may be an extreme example but a good way of illustrating how, in this stage, we can waste all the time we have spent in making a good impression and establishing our position as expert. The restaurant will have spent considerably on decor and on smart uniforms for the staff, invested in the skills of the chef and everything else that they need for a successful food business, but that's all been wasted because of the inability of the salesperson to ask questions and to listen to the customer.

That is why it's important to know that the two go together. You cannot have effective questioning without effective listening.

Questions

There are two general types of questions -- closed and open.

Closed questions are those that can be answered with a simple "yes" or "no" or another single word or a short phrase answer. The idea is that there are a set number of replies that one cannot stray from. "Which do you prefer?"

is a closed question because, in context, there may be only two choices being offered.

Examples include -
- "How old are you? "
- "Where do you live?"
- "What time is it?"

More relevant questions in sales are -
"Have you come to buy today?"
"Are you happy with your current supplier?"

Closed questions are good in their own way -
- They give you facts that you may need
- They are easy to answer (and ask!)
- The answer is quick
- They give the questioner absolute control of the conversation.

They can also bring the conversation/sales process to an end -
- "Is that a deal?"
- "Are you happy to proceed on these terms?"

However, they are limited in terms of being able to glean much in-depth information and encouraging customers to talk. It is certain that all salespeople will want to move towards the close, but to get to the most advantageous closing it is important to use the other sort of questions, the open question. Closed questions get customers to make decisions. This gets the customers closer to being ready to make a decision about the ultimate sale. We start with open questions and move toward closed questions at the customer's pace.

An open question is one where the answers received are likely to be longer. It is possible to ask a closed question and receive an unexpectedly long answer but a good open question actively encourages the other person to talk.

Open questions -
- Encourage the customer to think and reflect
- Invite the receiver to give their feelings and opinions on something.
- Also hands control of the conversation to the respondent

Examples of open questions include -
- "So what problems are you're having with your existing supplier?"
- "What are you looking to do with your new [product or service]?
- "What would you like us to do for you?"

Be careful of turning an open question into a closed one by adding a tag question. Compare the following -
- "How important is the color?"
- "Getting this product in a particular color is important to you, isn't it?"

The first question encourages the customer to explain why color is important – this may pass on some useful information for you such as the fact they have corporate colors they need to match – whilst the second version encourages a single word answer.

Open questions start with words such as what, why, how, describe etc…

Remember that your goal is getting people to talk. This will lead to you better meeting their needs. Losing control of the conversation can be scary but a well-placed open question, steered by well used closed questions can move your customer in the right direction. But be careful; a misplaced closed question can end the conversation so they are best avoided when the customer is in full flow.

These are the two main types of questions but there are other, sub-types of questions that can be either helpful or detrimental in this stage the process.

One type to be avoided are compound questions. These are not strictly different kinds of questions; they can be closed or open, but they are instances where a number of questions are being asked together.

Examples include -
- "What model are you looking at? What do you want it to do?"
- "What model and color are you wanting?"
- "What model, color, and price range you looking at?"

Compound questions are to be avoided because they can confuse the receiver. They can pick up on only one of the questions and forget about the rest, with you missing out on the chance to get this information. Compound questions are inefficient. They weaken your ability to gather information.

Other useful questions are funnel questions. These are ways that the questioner can manage the conversation, they are questions asked at a particular point in the conversation that guides the respondent, the customer, in a particular direction.

Examples include --
- "You mentioned option three before, why do you think that would help you?"
- "You said you're having a problem with X. Tell me more about that?"

These questions can gently guide a conversation in the right direction but be careful on doing this too early.

A second useful question when used at the right time is the leading question. Leading questions are something that we're sure you've seen on TV with judges instructing lawyers not to lead a witness! In fact, these can be very useful in a business situation.

> **REFLECTION POINT:**
>
> Can you think of some good open questions that would be appropriate for your work environment?
>
> It is often good to work on stock questions and to practice them on your mentors to see if they really promote conversation and information flow. Remember that the questions should be open but they should also be relevant.

Leading questions include
- "You would be happy to live with a delivery date of X, yes?"
- "You're willing to spend up to $X per unit, correct?"
- "Would you like to go ahead with package three?"

You will see that leading questions tend to be closed. A leading question is therefore useful in linking to a close.

Listening

We all listen – sometimes. Listening is how we all learn. It is how we pick up language when we are very young. It is an essential skill but this does not mean that we all listen well, that we have good listening skills or that we cannot learn to listen better.

How people respond to your questions and how you frame them is usually down to the process of listening. It is sometimes hard to listen but this is an important skill to learn. There are many subtle aspects to listening, including the quality of listening and how you are perceived to be listening. This can greatly affect the conversation and also how effectively you receive the information that the customer is giving you.

Listening should be effective. Listening can also be passive or active.

We will deal the latter two factors first.

Passive Listening

Passive listening is listening without reacting, allowing someone to speak without interruption, and not doing anything else at the same time. This might seem to be the right and respectful thing to do but, in fact, it can be off - putting, and it may make the customer think you're not listening. Also, consider the experience of being in a restaurant. Passive listening is 'hearing'. We hear the buzz of dozens of conversations going on simultaneously. However, if we focus our attention, we can 'listen' to a specific conversation and block out the rest of the background noise.

You should consider moving towards an active form of listening.

Active Listening

Active listening is reacting or doing something to show the other party that you have listened and understood.

With active listening you should -
- Give non-verbal clues to demonstrate that you are paying attention. These include nodding, making eye contact, making appropriate facial expressions, etc.
- Active listening can also be demonstrated by reflecting back on the main points made by the other party by summarizing what they have said.

Effective Listening

To listen effectively you should reduce any barriers that may exist to listening.

It is important to prepare beforehand --
- Try to ensure that you will have no interruptions before starting the conversation.
- Try to ensure that there are no extraneous or heavy background noises.
- Remember that people talk best in a relaxed, comfortable environment.
- Try not to have any physical barriers between you and the other person, such as a desk.

Whilst the customer is speaking --
- Focus on what they are saying. Don't be doing something else, including doodling or fiddling with a mobile phone.

- Make mental notes about what they are saying. If you find this difficult, ask the customer if it is okay to make a physical note.
- Try not only to listen to what is being said but also take note of the other person's body language as this will determine what mood they are in and how well your questions or contributions will be received.
- If something the customer says triggers something, an idea or a point you would like to make, but they are in mid-flow, giving you valuable information, avoid the temptation to interrupt. Keep a separate note of the point and be prepared to ask a question, or make a point at an appropriate time.
- Above all, avoid thinking about something else, or you will not be listening.

When the person has finished, when you summarize, don't repeat everything, just concentrate on the key points. Be as accurate as possible, even if the customer has said something which you disagree with.

> **REFLECTION POINT:**
>
> Are there any barriers to effective listening in your workplace? What could you do to improve things?

Discovery

As soon as you start talking, remember that the roles have swapped over. Always remember that listening is a very important tool in your toolbox. There is a tendency to talk too much and to listen too little in business. This is not a competition, you're not point scoring. This is listening and communicating with a purpose. That purpose is to meet the customer's needs and in doing so you should meet your needs by achieving a successful sale. There is a general rule of thumb that the customer should do approximately 70% of the talking. Closed ended questions tend to be longer than the responses to them, so the salesperson does the majority of the talking. Open questions are the key to keeping this ratio. A single question may be answered with an anecdote. This is what we want.

To conclude, it is perhaps important to remember things you should try to **avoid** at this stage in the process -

- There is always a temptation to try to impress or influence the customer. This is not the place to do it. You are trying to gather information that you do not know.
- Do not assume that you know what the customer is going to say.
- Do not fake attention. People are very good at spotting this.
- Listen properly not selectively – don't just hear what you want to hear.
- Do not bring personal concerns or problems to the process. You will not be able to concentrate properly.

At the end of this stage, if you have listened effectively and asked the right questions based upon what your customer has told you, you should have arrived at a solution that meets your client's needs – and you should be close to closing out the sale.

You should be well placed to start to pitch and negotiate the deal.

CHAPTER 5

PITCH AND BARGAINING

- In this chapter we will look at the process of pitching to the customer and bargaining to achieve the deal
- We stress that pitching is a 'salesman' term. Here, based on Selling With Authority, we take it that pitching is the same as proposing a solution.
- Although it is useful to know the theory involved in negotiation, the chapter continues the philosophy of Selling With Authority and encourages you to do the best deal for ALL parties
- Concepts such as distributive and integrative forms of negotiation are covered as well as BATNA, ZOPA and Reserve prices

---

We are now ready to tackle the area that a lot of sales books spend a lot of time on – pitching to a potential customer and bargaining – or negotiating – the deal. Like most things in this book we are, however, going to do things rather differently because in Selling with Authority our philosophy runs throughout and certainly doesn't stop at the point of negotiating the sale.

Selling with authority is solution selling rather than just selling a product or service. What we mean by that is that the aim is to work with the customer to produce a solution – perhaps a combination of products and services – that is both best for them and also for the company or organization you work for.

This can be seen to be an extension of the process that we have already introduced to you. You should have prepared well and known your product and the market inside out. You have made a good impression on the customer and built from that good first impression to establish yourself as an expert. You have started a conversation with purpose and discovered what your customer really needs. Now you need to take that to the next stage and agree to a mutually beneficial deal.

It is in this stage where your preparation and knowledge will really come into its own.

However, you will be able to pitch and negotiate properly only if you understand a little theory about negotiations. Ideally, if you follow the Selling with Authority model, the customer sees value in your proposal, and bargaining occurs to 'fine tune' the price / value gap.

You'll need to understand the difference between distributive and integrative negotiation and also look at concepts such as the BATNA (the Best Alternative to a Negotiated Agreement), the reservation price, and the ZOPA (the Zone of Possible Agreement).

Let's start with the two types of negotiation.

Distributive Negotiation

Distributive negotiation is whether the parties are competing over the distribution of a fixed sum of value. That sounds very complicated, but in fact it's essentially simple; the parties are haggling over the price of a product or service with the aim of achieving a deal. If no deal is agreed then no sale will take place. This is why distributive negotiations are sometimes referred to as a zero sum or win-lose negotiation type. Note in a 'zero-sum' negotiation, where the amount of the item being negotiated over is fixed, if I lose 1 and you gain 1, the sum of this is zero. Zero value is being built.

Integrative Negotiation

Integrative negotiation is a situation where parties co-operate to achieve the maximum benefits by integrating their interests into the agreement. Both parties are essentially trying to work together to achieve a common good. This is why integrative negotiations are referred to as win – win.

You can perhaps see the difference between the two.

With a distributive type of negotiation, the parties are adversarial. They are on different sides with each trying to achieve a win. With integrative approaches the parties are working more closely together. We believe you will appreciate that it is integrative type of negotiations which fits most successfully into the Selling with Authority type of approach. However, you may have to use aspects of distributive approach at some point in the negotiations to achieve a sale; therefore it is worthwhile looking at both methods in detail.

> **REFLECTION POINT:**
>
> What type of negotiations have you been involved in in your work up to now?
>
> Can you see areas where an integrative approach could have given you an advantage?

Distributive Negotiation Tactics

With distributive negotiations, there are certain tactics which are useful to know.

Distributive negotiations usually start by one of the parties making an offer. This is what is termed an Anchor offer. If it is the salesmen making the offer it is likely that they will start with a high anchor. This is very important as it psychologically sets the bargaining range. Quite often in distributive negotiations, the final price is strongly related to the initial anchor. However, the salesperson has to be careful not to overshoot. Pitching the anchor offer too high could make the other party leave the table before the bargaining has even begun because the prospective buyer may believe there is no chance of the price coming down to what they believe is a reasonable sum.

Distributive tactics are all about gaining power. The salesperson should not disclose any information to the other side, particularly not information that will weaken their position in any way. In particular they should not disclose the point at which they will walk away. On the other hand, the salesperson should be aiming to learn as much as possible about the other party's position. Knowledge is power. The salesperson will be seeking to exploit the situation that they have learned about the other party from the point of the first offer.

Another tactic that can be used in distributed negotiation is to make a counter offer, effectively setting a new anchor, attempting to reset the potential end position at a much lower or a much higher level.

It is sometimes important to bring objective data to the table, data that reinforces either an offer or a bid. The parties in it in distributive negotiations should prepare well and know in advance the concessions they are willing to make to achieve the deal.

The salesperson should also be aware of the effects and signals that movements from the initial offer have on the other party or, in turn, can inform themselves about the customer's position. If someone is making a large move from the initial offer (or counter offer) implies that there is a significant extra flexibility in the deal, that a lower price is possible. If the movements start to get smaller it is indicating that the party is getting close to reaching the final transaction price point. Think of this as fine tuning as opposed to a sculptor taking initial chunks from a stone. As salespeople, you should try to make only small corrections, and also anchor in your favor.

Distributive selling is connected with the traditional hard-sell. It is generally all about having the advantage. Whilst there is nothing wrong with trying to maximize a deal, the outcome can leave the other party – the customer – feeling hard done by. They may choose to go elsewhere after a particularly rough experience; the salesperson may have won the skirmish but lost the war and reduced the chances of repeat business.

Integrative Negotiation Tactics

The approach is quite different with integrative negotiations. As noted, the aim is to create value for both you and the other side. An integrative negotiations often involve concessions, hopefully from both sides. Each party will often concede certain terms but both sides should retain most, if not all, of what is important to them in the deal.

The tactics in integrative negotiations are very different. Unlike distributive selling, you should be prepared to provide significant information to the other side. This may include explaining the reasons behind wanting to make the deal. It is critical to the Selling with Authority model that an expert give ample information in order to PROVE knowledge and therefore authority. This begins, often, before negotiations even begin in the Discovery phase. Both sides will often need to talk about their real interests or business constraints and should be aiming to determine those of the other party.

You should be seeing echoes from the previous section. The best integrative negotiations involve the salesperson actively listening and to gain considerable empathy for the other side's perspectives, needs and interests, and adjusting their targets and assumptions based upon what they have learned – the actual pitch and negotiation part of the process is really just the second half of the process that determined the customer's needs. The link should effectively be seamless.

It can be a bit of a strange and perhaps alarming process for the traditional salesperson. Instead of jealously guarding information to gain the advantage, they are being asked to share it, perhaps revealing additional capabilities, resources or options that are available that the customer may not know about. Information gained and revealed should be used creatively to find options to aid the other party. This may involve trading off one feature against another. An example of this might be in selling printers to a customer. In the conversation you find they do bulk printing jobs, mainly in black and white – which suggests their best solution is a black and white laser printer. However they do need color on occasion, yet are reluctant to pay the extra cost for a good quality commercial grade color laser printer. Here it might be possible for the customer to be offered deeply discounted toner cartridges for their first year if they took the color option; the company would be trading off the profits from the consumables for a period in exchange for the higher initial sale, but in the long term both parties would benefit.

Although this may seem odd, remember this; A satisfied customer, one who thinks that they have got a good deal and value for money, who have been genuinely helped, is more likely to come back with repeat business or to recommend your company to someone else. Repeat business and referral business are more cost effective because it is done without expending the marketing budget on acquiring it. Less spend on marketing = higher profitability. Higher profitability = potentially higher benefits or rewards.

A win-win situation.

Reservation Price, ZOPA and BATNA

We look at some other concepts now which are useful to be aware of in negotiations. These are the reservation price, Zone Of Possible Agreement (ZOPA) and Best Alternative To a Negotiated Agreement (BATNA).

The reservation price is the walk away price, the point at which one of the parties will walk away. It's usually the least favorable point to agree to deal. It is the lower threshold at which an agreement can be made. This can be lower relative to the seller or higher relative to the buyer. Each will have a limit to what is acceptable to them. The buyer will not go above a certain price, the seller not below a certain price. If the price is too high, the buyer will leave. If the price offered is too low the seller will walk away.

The ZOPA represents the area of agreement, the range in which the deal can occur. Each parties reservation price determines the ZOPA. If the two parties' reservation prices do not overlap then no deal can be done. A good example of this is in Real Estate; A seller will market their property on a price based on advice from their realtor. A bid above this price is above this price is more likely to succeed but the seller is also likely to have a bottom line, a bid level that they might accept in order to achieve a quick sale. Everyone who views the property will be assessing how well the property meets their needs, what it is worth to them. Some will like the property enough to make a bid. This bid will be made based upon what the property is worth to them, not what the vendor says it is worth. Only if the bid is above the minimum price the seller will accept (ie: the reservation price) will it have a chance of being accepted. It does so because the bid has fallen within the ZOPA.

Closely related to this is the BATNA. This is the Best Alternative to a Negotiated Agreement. It is the fallback position if the negotiation does not happen or fails. You'll note that this is quite closely related to the reservation price. Is what you have to give up by not engaging in this transaction worth the cost of the transaction?

BATNA's can be weak or strong. If you have a strong BATNA, a strong fallback position, this greatly improves your negotiation position. You know that you have a strong alternative to fall back on if you cannot achieve what you want to. Conversely, having a weak BATNA gives you much less bargaining power. It is essential if you have a weak fallback position you don't let the other party know. We can return to the Real Estate example above to illustrate this; if the seller already holds a bid that is above their reservation price then they are in a very strong position with a second potential buyer who is keen on their property. The BATNA here is very strong and the seller can negotiate hard with this second party knowing that if they pitch the price too high they can revert to the original bidder. Contrast this with a seller who is being forced to sell because they can't keep up their mortgage payments. Their BATNA is extraordinarily weak; their alternative is to give the keys back to the lender. The last thing the seller should admit to anyone viewing the property is the financial position that they are in.

If you do have a weak BATNA there are three things to do.

Firstly is to simply improve your BATNA. If you know you are weak you need to improve your fallback position if at all possible. This should be part of your preparation. Even having a weak BATNA is still better than the alternative however. What is the alternative? To have no fallback position. If you have no fallback position then this is an extraordinarily weak position to enter into negotiation. Often, being forced into a deal is opportune for only one party - the person not forced into the transaction.

The second way of negotiating if you have a weak BATNA is to try to identify the other parties BATNA.

You will do this by intelligent questioning. As with many things, knowledge about the other side's position is power.

The third technique if you have a weak BATNA is to do everything to weaken the other side's BATNA. Again you will do this by intelligent questioning but also by intelligent point making to undermine the other side's position. In the Real Estate example above, a buyer should try to determine what position the seller is in and also ask how long the property has been on the market and how many viewings there have been. If the seller is desperate to move and the property has been on the market for a long time then the buyer knows that the seller's BATNA is weak. Likewise, the seller should ask questions of the potential buyer; why they are looking to move, do they have a house to sell first?

The quality of information that you can gain is very important otherwise you can only go into the negotiation with a fuzzy idea of what your fallback position is. You certainly need to know the minimum threshold to negotiate a deal, and if possible, how flexible the other party is going to be. You need to know what they will trade off to obtain what they want. Again this requires a lot of intelligence gathering to achieve.

The reservation price, the ZOPA and the BATNA are important to be aware of in all negotiations, but it should be stressed that in the desired integrative negotiation path, the free flow of information and desire to meet a mutually beneficial agreement means that the salesperson is not trying to achieve a position of power.

> **REFLECTION POINT:**
>
> How do you think you could find out details of the customer's BATNA?
>
> See if you can come up with some subtle ways of doing this.

Pitching and Bargaining in Selling with Authority

You will actually have many of the tools already available to you at the point negotiations are opened if you have embraced the entirety of the process; indeed the negotiation phase will be seamless with the discovery phase; one should flow into the other.

There are things to stress however.

If you know your product and the market inside out you should be able to recognize the customer's needs and provide solutions and reasoned arguments as to why they would be successful. For example, if you are selling cars you could offer the option of power windows by explaining their convenience, or air-conditioning even in temperate climates for the system's advantages in demisting. If you are selling alarm systems you should know the technical details of the product but also the impact it would have on home insurance premiums. Everything should be focused on the customer's needs. If you are in the cell phone business and you find that your customer makes only phone calls, a 4G package will greatly exceed what they need. If they need access to data such as presentations or real-time stock movements, or if they use their cell phone for entertainment such as gaming and movies, then the home broadband speeds on-the-go would be ideal. The list is as endless as the number of salespersons and the markets they serve.

This does not mean that the salesperson should not think laterally to maximize revenue. There are times, for example, when you could consider bundling things together and offering an overall discount. Consider a company that is offering three products that each cost $100. The total cost is of course $300. A budget conscious customer might try to save money by omitting one of the products entirely, leaving the business with a total revenue of $200. If you offered them the total bundle with, say a 10% discount, that would mean total revenue of $270. How would you know that the customer was budget conscious but would be tempted by a deal? By the integrated process of discover and the dialogue of an integrative negotiation recommended by Selling with Authority!

Because there are so many different selling circumstances it is impossible to give a fully comprehensive set of examples to illustrate this section, however we can state with confidence that if you adopt the entire philosophy of Selling with Authority, you will find pitching and negotiating a natural extension of what has come before.

CHAPTER 6

POST-SALE

- In this chapter we will look at the importance of the period after the sale has been made
- We will explore the area of Customer Relationship Management (CRM) and how this fits into the Selling With Authority philosophy
- At the end of the chapter you will understand the importance of customer retention and how you should aim to build an on-going relationship with your customer

---

The post-sale area has developed greatly over recent years. Indeed a whole new industry has developed out of it – CRM – Customer Relationship Management. CRM is a complex and far reaching subject which could quite easily be the subject of a book in its own right. As such, its detail is beyond the scope of this book. However, its importance can be underlined by the alternative interpretation of the acronym; Continual Revenue Multiplier! Although this is usually said in jest it is, like the best jokes, based on an underlying truth. This truth also fits in well with the philosophy of Selling with Authority.

A sale is only a momentary point in the sales process; it does not last long in its own right. The sale is the goal of the sales process but the important thing to remember is that it is not the endpoint. The ideal, the thing that makes your investment in time and knowledge truly worthwhile and efficient, is if that relationship continues and if more sales flow from it.

The customer development process

The importance of this can perhaps best be explained by looking at figure 6, below.

Figure 6.1 The Customer Development Process

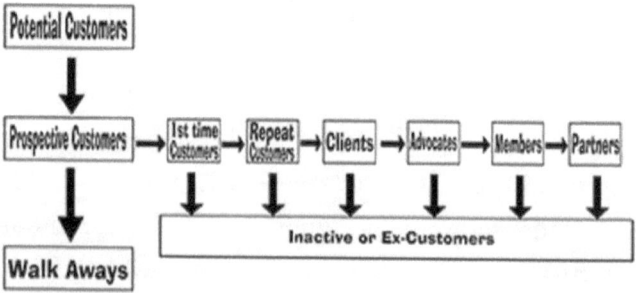

This is a really good visual representation of the sales process. What we have done in the first part of the book is concentrated on the process that is shown on the left hand side of the diagram; finding and identifying potential customers, attracting them so that they become prospective customers and do not walk away and turning them into first time customers by finding out their needs and providing solutions that meet them. If the process ends there then it is quite possible that this new customer will walk away after only one sale has been made and they will become inactive or ex-customers.

This is a waste. It is inefficient.

It is generally accepted that, on average, it costs 5 – 10 times as much to attract a new customer as it does to keep a current customer satisfied. It is this harsh economic fact that is the simple reason why CRM has become so important and why it has developed into a career path and an industry in its own right. CRM is all about attracting, retaining and building long term relationships. It is all about converting that customer into a repeat customer, then this customer becomes a client, one that the company has a long term, on-going and usually two-way relationship with. Ideally this may move on; the customer will hopefully become an advocate for your company or product, referring you on to other potential customers and, ultimately, may even partner with you.

> **REFLECTION POINT:**
>
> In your current role are you spending more time with new customers or repeat customers?
>
> Who is it easiest to deal with and do business with; new or existing customers?

This is the importance of an on-going relationship. Losing a customer through bad CRM means losing not only the entire stream of purchases that the customer would make over the lifetime of the relationship but also the free marketing of referrals and the lifetime purchases made by these referred customers.

You may be reading this and thinking; "Well that's fine, but my job is sales. CRM is not for sales people, it's for others, people who are paid to do it, or for the management. All my job is is to get the process going."

That may be so but consider this.

If you are working for an organization who concentrates only on the left hand side of the diagram, on sales and marketing only and neglecting the right-hand side, the CRM area, then each of the sales you achieve will be much more expensive overall than those of your rivals who consider the whole process. This will mean that your company will be less profitable than this rival. This equates to being able to pay lower salaries and smaller bonuses. It also means that your company will be more vulnerable to changing market conditions. In a downturn we all know that finding customers gets even harder, that money spent on marketing gets less effective. Those long-term, repeat business customers who come back to you are even more important. Simply put, the company who puts more effort into CRM and long-term relationships will be much more likely to survive in the long run.

The default thought behind "marketing" is about how to attract new customers (potential customers), but we don't really think about marketing to our existing customer base. This might involve offering a new product or service that our existing customers don't know about or offering some kind of loyalty based bonus or additional service available only to existing customers.

> **REFLECTION POINT:**
>
> What can you do in your workplace to offer added value or additional services to your existing customers that will improve the chances of them being retained?

The other thing to consider is this – and this takes us straight back to Selling With Authority; we have shown you the advantages of you becoming an expert, someone the customer will want to consult, look to for advice and knowledge. Typically experts – lawyers, doctors, marketing and advertising professionals, architects etc. - do not have customers, they have CLIENTS, i.e. the relationship is well to the right-hand side of the diagram. Selling with Authority done properly simply requires you to have an on-going relationship with your customer.

As a salesperson it is well worth taking on some of the CRM functins. It is clearly in your interests.

'Old' selling versus 'New' selling

As we have already mentioned, there is an awful lot written on the topic of CRM, far too much to do justice to in this book. However, there are some basic principles that can be understood and followed which should be used to manage client relationships post-sale which we will cover here.

For a start, the whole ethos of sales in general has changed, and the most successful organizations have recognized this and embraced the changes:

Old Selling	New Selling
Mass customers	Tailored to each customer
Selling driven by supply, pushing what has been produced	Demand driven sales – customer pulls production
Transaction focused	

Adversarial negotiations	Focus is on relationships
Adversarial negotiations	Professional/ Partnership negotiations
Separate sales/after-sales/supply functions	Integrated roles
Deliberately obscure pricing	Transparent pricing
Sales are a time consuming process	Efficient and short duration

> **REFLECTION POINT:**
>
> What is your organization like? Is its model 'old' selling or 'new'?
>
> If it has a lot of the features of 'old' selling, what could you do to change this?

Having a longer, deeper, more genuine relationship with a customer/client is the basis of good CRM but is also a feature of Selling with Authority. Both yourself and the organization you work for should be focused on the customer and their needs. It is important to look at what you are doing – are you and your business actually offering programs and projects that are responding to your customer's needs? Or are you just doing what is most convenient to you? This can be a difficult question but it is fundamental and it should be answered honestly.

One thing to consider is where after-sales are positioned in your organization. Too often in 'old selling', after-sales relationship was conducted at the wrong level:

It is natural in a business that sales are accorded a high priority in the hierarchy. Sales can take place at any level from executive level down to specialized front line staff – often specialized sales staff.

Traditionally, however, after-sales service tends to get pushed down the hierarchy. You can understand the thinking; sales and management is specialist, expensive. They are best moved onto the next potential lead to try to convert that to a new sale.

Figure 6.2 The Sales Function in a typical Organizations Hierarchy

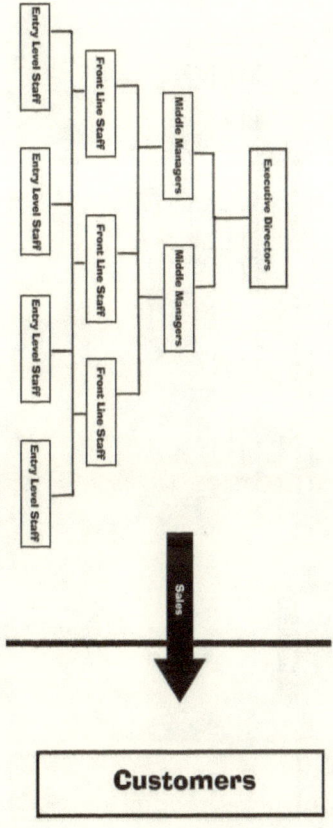

Figure 6.3 The After-Sales Function in some Organization's Hierarchy

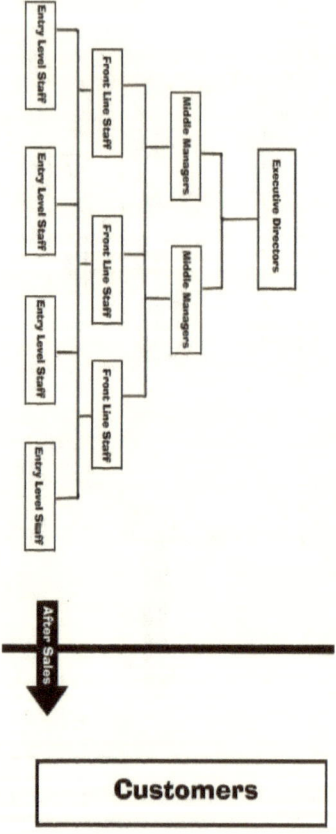

The problem with this thinking – which does make perfect sense – is that these staff are the cheapest for good reason. They lack experience. They lack knowledge. They may be college graduates on their first placement or on short term contracts with little stake or interest in the development of the company. They will be well meaning and eager, but what kind of experience will the customer obtain? You have invested considerable effort in establishing yourself as an expert with unrivaled product knowledge, someone that the customer respects; this situation is one that could totally destroy this trust. It does need careful management.

Practical on-going customer relationships

Of course, the big practical problem for most sales people is time. Very few sales people have the luxury of the time to both fully fulfill their sales function and to cultivate their existing clients. There is, of course, the traditional client relationship builders that mix 'play' with work – corporate golf days, wine tastings and the like – but these tend to be too expensive and infrequent to fully rely on. Luckily we have been helped by technology; CRM does not have to be always face-to-face. A company's website is increasingly important in projecting the image of the company and in communicating with a customer. We are helped by trends in behavior; most people's first reaction when wanting to know about a product today is to go to the company's website. The website is a vitally important portal to both the company in general and also in terms of CRM.

Have a look at a range of websites, not only in your company's field but in other industries too. Outside online retailers, you will, most likely, be struck by one thing; how little overt selling is done. Most good websites are all about information, information that is helpful to the customer, telling them about new trends, or new legislation that might affect them.

Step back a moment and consider; what does that sound like? The companies on these websites are positioning themselves as experts in their field, knowledgeable, reliable, a place a customer can go to get solid information. If they find this they will come back time and time again. On some of these visits they will hopefully buy. It is just the same process as you strive to do face-to-face to establish your status as expert and for the same reason.

Some companies go too far in this however, relying on the website too much to deliver their CRM. There is still the need for more personal, two way communication. Again we are aided by technology; a personal, direct, tailored e-mail backed up by the occasional phone call keeps up the long term relationship – with one proviso of course; you are not always pestering for sales. That is a guaranteed way to have your customer avoid you. If you come with useful information – a report, news of a seminar – or a sincere inquiry as to how the product is performing for the customer, or even asking for feedback and advice about how the product could be improved, then the more likely it is that the relationship is being built.

We have already said that we will not be looking in detail at CRM theories and concepts but there is one we would like to consider, one you may well have heard of: the 20/80 rule.

The 20/80 rule is a rough rule of thumb. It states that in most organizations the top 20% of the customers generate 80% of the profit. It goes on to say that the bottom 10-20% of the customers actually reduce profits whilst the bulk of the customers – 60-70% - just about break even, the revenue generated is just balanced by the costs of obtaining them. The logic then is to concentrate most of the CRM effort on the 20% at the top because this will maximize returns.

There is obvious logic in this but it also worth questioning whether this is truly sensible. What are the effects going to be on the 80% of customers who have little time devoted to them? They might feel neglected and unwanted. They may well walk away. They certainly will not do that most important thing a customer can do for you; refer and recommend. This may be the logical thing to do in 'old' selling, with the adversarial approach, but taking a more intelligent, discovery led approach could find ways of re-packaging and restructuring a deal that could take a non-performing customer into that top 20.

You don't know until you try.

CRM is all about building genuine, long term relationships. Just the same in fact as is the entire philosophy of Selling With Authority.

CHAPTER 7

KNOWLEDGE, SKILLS, ABILITIES AND OTHER FACTORS

- In this chapter we will bring together all the components of Selling With Authority
- This will enable you to establish a road map as to the personal development you will need to develop the skill-sets to maximize the benefits to you

---

We started this book with a few statements:
- We said that this book alone would not turn you into a super-salesperson overnight but would rather give you the skill-sets and the way of thinking that would set you on the right path

- We asserted that Selling with Authority would give you advantages outside of the narrow field of selling but also in your general life – indeed that this was a way of simulating the characteristics of 'the success gene'
- We also said that you would finish the book with more questions than you had when you started!

That might seem a little unfair; it almost sounds like we are leaving you to sink or swim. This is absolutely not the case; all we are saying is that the principles of Selling With Authority go far deeper than a simple formula that can be learned and picked up in a single seminar or through reading one book. It takes work by the individual and the details of the work will depend upon the individual and their circumstances. You, the individual, will have to formulate and ask the questions that are pertinent to yourself to best adopt the principles of Selling With Authority for yourself. Think of Selling With Authority as a skeleton or framework – it is up to you how you flesh it out or cover it. This chapter will try to suggest ways forward to identify areas that you can work on.

What we have now is the full picture of Selling With Authority. It is the first chance that we have had to see the whole picture – it is after all a PROCESS not a POINT IN TIME model – and see how it all knits together, each stage helping the next:

Selling With Authority: The Overall Picture

> **REFLECTION POINT:**
>
> What model is your own work environment like in regards to on-going customer relationship?

To see the full picture is really important because it gives an understanding of how integrated Selling With Authority is. Each stage is as important as the last; none can be neglected. Developing skills and knowledge in one area enhances the others and eases the transition from stage to stage. It is an in-depth integrated way of improving your ability as a salesperson.

Strategy and Preparation

This is the stage in which the groundwork for the entire process is made. It is where you gain the knowledge about the product, market and industry that you work in. It is where you gain an understanding of what your potential customers do and what their needs are. It prepares you for being an EXPERT that customers will want to consult.

This preparation means that you can move confidently into the next phase, making it easier to engage a customer and gain their confidence.

Locate and Engage Customers

Ensuring that you have made a good first impression on your potential customer, this is where you engage and impress them. They may bring preconceptions with them, be on their guard against the hard-sell. Your knowledge and approach will challenge this view and lead them to recognize you as someone who can help and advise. Ensuring that you have made a good first impression on your potential customer, this is where you engage and impress them. They may bring preconceptions with them, be on their guard against the hard-sell. Your knowledge and approach will challenge this view and lead them to recognize you as someone who can help and advise.

Discovery

This is where you find out what the customer's needs are. You need to use the sometimes conflicting skills of listening and questioning. As an expert you should be listening a lot, letting the customer speak and pass information onto you, using questions sparingly to guide the process.

If you have done this well, this and your prior knowledge will have guided you to a solution.

Pre-Sale

Once you have a solution that you know will meet the customer's needs you can then pitch with confidence to them. The negotiations should be integrative, not adversarial, with a goal of achieving the best result for both parties.

This can be hard in an environment which is all about goals and achieving sales but it should ensure an on-going relationship with the customer.

And once again, what you have done in the earlier stages will not stop here but will lead naturally on to the post-sales relationship.

Post-Sale

If you have impressed the client with your knowledge and understanding, and if they feel that the deal done is fair, they will be much more likely to both come back and recommend you to others. This is a good start to the CRM process and is highly efficient for the company given the expense of gaining new customers.

It should also be clear that, to be successful, you will need to develop different skills for each different stage. Some skills are common throughout – being able to see things through the client's lens for example (sometimes known as empathy) - whilst others are more stage specific. To understand the skills you need to work on we have split up the Selling With Authority process into its components and provided comments and suggestions as to personal development areas to concentrate on.

Preparation and Strategy

The skills here are somewhat different from those later in the process where you can be outgoing, extrovert and open. Here you need to use the quieter, more patient, diligent and introverted skills of research. You will also need the skills to think laterally and to see problems from different viewpoints – you will almost certainly need to try to see things from the customer's perspectives to see what they need from the product or service rather than from the company's need which is to sell.

Locate and Engage Customers

To start with you will need an eye for detail, for presentation and concentration – as well as an ability to see things from the customer's viewpoint. This will enable you to make that good first impression at all times. You will then need to build on this, which will require the development of confidence and authority. You will also need to develop skills of empathy – to see things from the customer's point of view and understand their position.

Discovery

Empathy is again important in the discovery phase – you need to be able to step into the customer's shoes to understand their needs – but the soft-skills that need to be practised and developed here are those connected with listening and questioning.

Pre-Sale

Once again, empathy is important – it is a common theme that runs throughout – but you will need to work on yours skills of negotiation. The skills you have in this area may need to be re-learned and refocused. Traditional selling stresses negotiation as competition, with the salesperson encouraged to maximise the sales and get an advantage over the customer. Selling With Authority encourages a more integrative, partnering approach that encourages a longer-term solution that fosters a client/professional type relationship rather than a customer/salesperson short term one.

Post-Sale

The skills to be developed here are all about relationship building, about continuing a dialogue, and about showing interest without becoming intrusive and irritating. This is sometimes a different form of dialogue than occurs earlier and may need practising. You will also need to develop non-verbal communication skills, particularly those around new technology – electronic communication, web skills and knowledge and perhaps in the use of social media for business – twitter, Linkedin and Facebook can be good ways of maintaining links with customers.

The review of these skill-sets is one of the most important things you can do. We all have a tendency to favor the things that we do well and concentrate on them. It is a natural thing to do, everyone likes the feeling of doing something that they know they are good at; it feels safe, it gives you security and – naturally – it is easier to succeed at these things. It is much less comfortable and natural to attempt to do something that we know we are not good at. It feels wrong and there are expectations of failure – which are often realized! Yet how can any of us develop as people if we don't push ourselves to improve areas where we know we have weaknesses? This is why an honest audit of how your skill-set matches against the requirements of Selling with Authority is important.

Whilst it is hard to face up to our weaknesses it is also sometimes hard to recognize them ourselves. Sometimes our viewpoint about ourselves is distorted, sometimes it is simply wrong! It is not our fault; we cannot always be too objective about ourselves. This is where your mentors – particularly your horizontal mentors, those at the same level as you – are particularly useful. They should have been chosen because they know you, and what you do, particularly well. Put figure 7.2 in front of them, or perhaps list the skill-sets, and ask them to be honest about how you do with each in their opinion.

> **REFLECTION POINT:**
>
> Look carefully at Figure 7.2 In what areas are you relatively strong in these skill-sets? Perhaps more importantly, where are you weakest? What areas do you need to work on?

Once you have done that, what do you do next? Well the answer has to be to strive to improve them. The best way is using your individual business plan.

Knowledge, Skills, Abilities and Other Factors

If you remember, we introduced the idea of your individual business plan in chapter 2, and the SMART goals that were in it in it. To remind you, a SMART goal is:

Specific – what EXACTLY are you going to improve?
Measurable – how will you measure progress in your improvement?
Actionable – what specific actions will you take to improve each factor?
Resourced – what tools do you have to make the improvements to each factor?
Time-bound - how often will you revisit your progress or what deadlines have you set?

Improving your skill-sets in the areas that have been identified as weaknesses is most definitely a great SMART goal.

The other thing to remember about skill-sets, even the ones that you are currently strong in, is that they do need maintaining. The best business people, like the best athletes, constantly need to maintain and practice what they do well to keep doing well. Complacency is a terrible characteristic to have. An example might be someone who used to be the office wiz on Excel ten years ago. He was the person everyone went to to sort out their spreadsheet problems. Since then they have moved onto other things, perhaps taken on a management function. On their resume it probably stills says 'Excel expert' but if faced with the software as it exists today you would probably find that they were completely lost with all the new features. Think of social media, of Facebook and Twitter – ten years ago they simply didn't exist; what you know about them today will probably not be valid in 12 months time.

It is important to remember that maintaining what you have is as at least as important as acquiring something new – this maxim applies to customers as much as it applies to skill-sets and knowledge.

Some Conclusions

We made some big claims in the introduction to this book. We said that this was not just a narrow book about sales but rather that it had a much wider application; that life was fundamentally about selling – ideas, concepts, ourselves – and that anything that could improve that was going to give us benefits. We even talked about 'The success gene' and how Selling With Authority could give the strong impression that you had it.

How have we done? Do our claims stack up?

To be consistent, it is difficult to be objective about oneself. An assessment of strengths and weaknesses best comes from a third party, so it really should be you that is the judge of this! What we can say is that if you take on the principles of Selling with Authority in your work environment you will certainly find some of the benefits spilling over into other parts of your life. And consider this; who in your life have you turned to when you really needed advice or an opinion, when things were really serious and you needed someone sound? The person you went to was probably knowledgeable, they were able to empathize with you, see the problem through your eyes. They almost certainly listened, asked sensible questions, weighed things up and then proposed a solution for you or at least suggested a way forward. They probably also said that they would be there for you and would try to help again in the future if you needed it.

We all want someone like that in our lives. Often it is a parent or an older sibling, or some other relative or friend, someone who has a stake in, someone who we know we can trust and rely on.

Look at that description. That Mom or Dad, Brother or Sister, Uncle or Aunt is displaying all of the characteristics that a customer would like in you – that go-to person that they can trust, it is exactly the characteristics that Selling with Authority stresses. And if you apply them in more general circumstances then you become the natural 'go-to' person, the person that everyone turns to to provide solutions.

And to complete the circle, that does rather sound like someone who has The Success Gene!

www.ingramcontent.com/pod-product-compliance
Lightning Source LLC
Chambersburg PA
CBHW030853180526
45163CB00004B/1560